A SMALL
SHARE OF WISDOM

By Sayer Broughton

BOOKS BY SAYER BROUGHTON

A Small SHARE OF WISDOM

PLEASING MINDS

HERE IS FINE

LEAVE THIS WORLD ALONE

A GENTLE TOUCH: Massage Poems

IT'S STILL ME

A SMALL
SHARE OF WISDOM

By Sayer Broughton

Open Look Books

A Small Share of Wisdom

Available at Amazon, Kindle, Barnse & Noble
& fine bookstores everywhere

Book Design by Jeremy King

Cover Illustration by Lilly Ross

ISBN 978-0-912350-61-5

"I often quote myself.
It adds spice to my conversation."

— *George Bernard Shaw*

Introduction:

A Small Share of Wisdom is a collection of my own thoughts and ideas, many of which, nearly all, spilled from me onto sticky notes. Is there really wisdom here? I would hope some, but wisdom is a powerful—and perhaps too grand a term, one to be carefully employed. In another sense, this book is really a personal reminiscence of several journeys, my own and others, and a miscellany of a writer's sentiments.

This book then follows late-night murmerings—or dreamscapes—where I'd awaken in the morning to find a scribble sitting there on the bed-stand. Ah, what would any writer do without sticky notes? It was a joy, finally, gathering these little pieces of paper that sometimes would startle when they first magically arrived. I hope that this compendium, wise or not, serves as a mild food for thought or an occasioned remembrance of heart.

— *Sayer Broughton*

"Why did we empty?
So we could fill back up."

"Sometimes you need to immerse yourself in cold water, to feel the heat again."

"You can only live
the same life twice."

"I don't blame other people for what we've done together."

"Positive is a bubble,
negative is not real:
Step into the middle to
see how you feel."

"Once was a family of geese. They parted directions. A wind came, their flock blew apart."

"Don't be who you want to be. Be somebody who wants to be you."

"The more times one stays the same, the more times one changes."

"Don't be who you are, you already are that. Be who you've known you were before you decided."

"Why don't you ask for what you want? Because you'll get it?"

"Nothing matters except
for what matters."

"One is for you, two is for me, three is for us. What else can that spell but magic?"

"Consistency wasn't 1 + 1,
but it was 2."

"Wanting to be needed so much, you forget yourself."

"Why are we so sad for people that are alive, as if they are dead?"

"Do you really want to control somebody and then make them into something they are impossibly not?"

"Yes, I will wear designer fashions and write a poem about a poem, then dance."

"You had to think you know people."

"Follow truth, it is alighting everywhere."

"Gotta go to the origins
to understand."

"You must win, when
you do not lose."

"One plan to change is to
do the same."

"You have already lived tomorrow, so why are you telling me today's weather?"

"Peace wants the answer;
it is in the next breath."

"Nothing is for nothing. So you did it all for nothing?"

"Begin by starting to live
one step behind another."

"Multiply yourself, then divide by you and you alone."

"Don't ever be. Just look as if you're not doing anything."

"Where is one truth,
when no one listens?"

"Today was a memory
of this I forgot to do."

"Good is created by people who perceive it."

"Don't take anything personally from people you do not respect."

"Don't be a fool, be foolish. It's foolproof."

"Stop being yourself. Be
the wish you wanted."

"I will cry no longer for
my own death."

"Pay this world with
creativity."

"Ask yourself one question, 'Who lives with you now?'"

"When did we lose our sense of humility?
I mean humor."

"Are you going to be the very stars above? If so, what else are you going to look at?"

"Did the scenery make
the man or did the ocean
drift it all to sea?"

"Be amused by small
things unnoticed."

"Try, but don't try."

"We defeat ourselves
through each other."

"The bridge is not the tower."

"Let's build a pond, so
we can write poetry."

"If we follow the horseshit,
we can find the horse."

"Let pain decide your next course of action and you may have missed the message."

"Being good takes work."

"Receiving light from dark intention is losing before the battle has even been won."

"Give me some more of
that vague realness."

"Anger wasn't an ending;
it was a gateway."

"Refuse to allow other people to abuse you by abusing yourself."

"It was only a word, a combination of sounds until someone gave music to it."

"It's as if you have to think, to know people."

"Look beyond your thoughts."

"You don't win by being afraid to lose."

"You got what you want:
a belief that might
never come true."

"Believe in me, I absolutely know nothing."

"Map it out, distant views."

"How many hand
gestures made it later
too much to do?"

"Move to the one who is."

"Just to revisit what we have known our whole lives."

"Sometimes you live and other times you forget to."

"If you leave a little
extra, don't expect to
come back later for it."

"From all great acts,
some semblance
remains."

"You haven't been;
you still are."

"Live toward the present."

"A great test of life:
seeing who's at your
side when you arrive."

Made in the USA
Columbia, SC
18 September 2019